D0765710

A to Z Germany

BY JEFF REYNOLDS

children's press®

A Division of Scholastic Inc.
New York Toronto London Auckland Sydney
Mexico City New Delhi Hong Kong
Danbury, Connecticut

Consultant: Irina Burns
Series Design: Marie O'Neill
Photo Research: Candlepants Incorporated
Language Consultant: Miles Edward Rowe, M.A.

For Jaime, Kelly, Casey, Carrie, A. J., and Brady
– J.R

Amerikaner recipe provided by Christina Hesse

The photos on the cover show a swan (top left), Schloss Moritzburg near Dresden (top right), a nutcracker (bottom right), and a boy in Bavarian dress (bottom center).

Photographs © 2004: AllSport USA/Getty Images/Ross Kinnaird: 28 bottom; Animals Animals: 26 (Henry Ausloos), 4 (J & C Sohns), 5 top right (Peter Weimann); AP/Wide World Photos: 13 left; Corbis Images: 12 top (AFP), 14 (Archivo Iconografico, SA), 9 right (Dave Bartruff), 15 right, 38 (Bettmann), 15 left (Barney Burstein/Burstein Collection/„ 2004 Artists Rights Society (ARS), New York/VG Bild-Kunst, Bonn), 17 left (Christie's Images), 27 right (The Corcoran Gallery of Art), 13 right, 36 left (Owen Franken), cover top left (Darrell Gulin), 24 bottom (Wolfgang Kaehler), 17 right, 24 top, 31 top, 35 bottom right (Bob Krist), 22 (James Marshall), 5 bottom (Naturfoto Honal), 34 top (Jose F. Poblete), 18, 19 (Premium Stock), 12 bottom (Reuters NewMedia Inc.), cover bottom right (Royalty-Free), 35 top right (Gregor Schmid), 25 bottom (Peter Turnley), 30 (Nik Wheeler), 8 bottom right (Adam Woolfitt), 32; Envision Stock Photography Inc.: 35 left (Michael Howell), 11 (George Mattei); Index Stock Imagery: 7 (Peter Adams), 27 left (IT Stock International), 29 (Thomas Winz); Mary Evans Picture Library: 31 bottom; Peter Arnold Inc./Helga Lade/Schultz: 28 top; Photo Researchers, NY/Hans Reinhard/OKAPIA: 5 top left; PictureQuest/Joshua Ets-Hokin/Photodisc: 8 left; Stone/Getty Images: 6 bottom (Fernand Ivaldi), cover top right (Wilfried Krecichwost), 6 top (Rohan), 10, 16 (Michael Rosenfeld); Superstock, Inc./Steve Vidler: cover center, 8 top right, 25 top, 37 bottom; Taxi/Getty Images/Ron Chapple: 9 left; The Image Bank/Getty Images/Andreas Stirnberg: 23; The Image Works: 37 top (Hideo Haga/HAGA), 36 bottom right (Joerg Mueller), 33 (Topham), 34 bottom (Charles Walker/Topfoto), 36 top right (Masakatsu Yamazaki/HAGA).
Map by XNR Productions

Library of Congress Cataloging-in-Publication Data

Reynolds, Jeff E., 1958-
   Germany / by Jeff Reynolds.
      p. cm. — (A to Z)
Contents: Animals – Buildings – Cities – Dress – Exports – Food – Government – History – Important people – Jobs – Keepsakes – Land – Map – Nation – Only in Germany – People – Question – Religion – School and sports – Transportation – Unusual Places – Visiting the Country – Window to the past – X-tra special things – Yearly festivals – Z – Let's Explore More.
Includes bibliographical references and index.
   ISBN 0-516-23654-7 (lib. bdg.)   0-516-25071-X (pbk.)
1. Germany—Juvenile literature. I. Title. II. Series.
   DD17.R49 2004
   943—dc22
                                              2004003281

34569854 2/07

1 2 3 4 5 6 7 8 9 10 R 13 12 11 10 09 08 07 06 05 04

Contents

Animals

Wolves are characters in many German folktales, such as Little Red Riding Hood.

Germany has wolves, wild boars, **chamois**, white storks, and other animals. Not many wolves are found in Germany today.

4

Chamois

Wild boars have dangerous tusks.

Wild boars are members of the pig family. They can still be found in the forests of southeastern Germany.

Chamois and storks live in Germany, too. Chamois are a type of antelope. They live on the rocky slopes of Germany's mountains. Small **herds** are made up of mothers and their young.

There are many storks in Europe. Towns in Germany receive special honors if they can get these large birds to build their nests nearby.

White storks are considered good luck.

5

Brandenburg Gate in Berlin

A modern bank building
in Munich

Buildings

One of the best-known attractions in Germany is the Brandenburg Gate in Berlin. It is a symbol of many things in Germany's history, both good and bad. During the time when Germany was divided into two separate nations, the Brandenburg Gate was a symbol of sadness. Germans could not cross from one side of the gate to the other. Today, Germany is a united country. The Brandenburg Gate has become a symbol of Germany's pride.

Look at all the tall buildings in Frankfurt. Can you think of any other cities that have tall buildings?

Cities

German cities are a mix of old and new. Frankfurt is Europe's most important banking center. There are other important cities like Berlin (Germany's capital), Frankfurt, Hamburg, and Cologne. Cologne was Germany's largest city during the **Middle Ages**. It will be 2,000 years old soon! Hamburg is Germany's second-largest city and the country's most important port. There are more bridges in Hamburg than in any other city in the world.

Girls in dirndl dresses

Wool sweaters like this one keep children warm in the cool mountain climate.

Dress

During holidays and festivals, many Germans enjoy dressing in traditional German clothing. When they are not celebrating, they dress like people in the United States do.

Look at all the different clothing Germans wear! **Lederhosen** are short pants that are worn by men and boys. They are usually made of leather. Hats made of green felt that are decorated with feathers are also common, especially in the Bavarian region.

Women and girls often wear **dirndl** dresses. A dirndl is made up of a vest-like top that is laced or buttoned snuggly over a full skirt. It is worn with a loose-fitting white blouse and an apron.

Older people in Bavaria often dress in traditional clothing year-round.

9

Automobiles are
one of Germany's
top exports.

Exports

Germany is the world's third-largest producer of automobiles. Names connected with German automaking include Porsche, BMW, Volkswagen, Audi, and Mercedes-Benz. Other exports for which Germany is known are steel, iron, chemicals, medicine, wine and beer, ships, **porcelain**, toys, and paper. Most German exports find their way to the countries that make up the **European Union**.

Amerikaner Recipe

WHAT YOU NEED:
- 1/2 cup margarine
- 2/3 cup granulated sugar
- 2 eggs
- 1-1/2 cups all-purpose flour
- 2 teaspoons baking powder
- 4 tablespoons milk
- 2 tablespoons powdered sugar
- 1 tablespoon water

HOW TO MAKE IT:
Preheat oven to 390 °F. Spray or grease cookie sheet. Beat together margarine, granulated sugar, and eggs until fluffy. Add to this mixture the flour, baking powder, and milk. Mix well. Spoon onto cookie sheet in clumps about 2 tablespoons large. Leave plenty of space between cookies. Bake for approximately 25 minutes, or until cookies begin to turn brown around the edges. When cooled, drizzle the cookies with icing made from the powdered sugar and water. Cocoa can also be added to the icing.

Food

German cooks are known for baking many kinds of breads and pastries. Berliners are sugary, donut-like treats named for the capital city. Amerikaners are cookies that became popular after World War II. Ask an adult to help you make them.

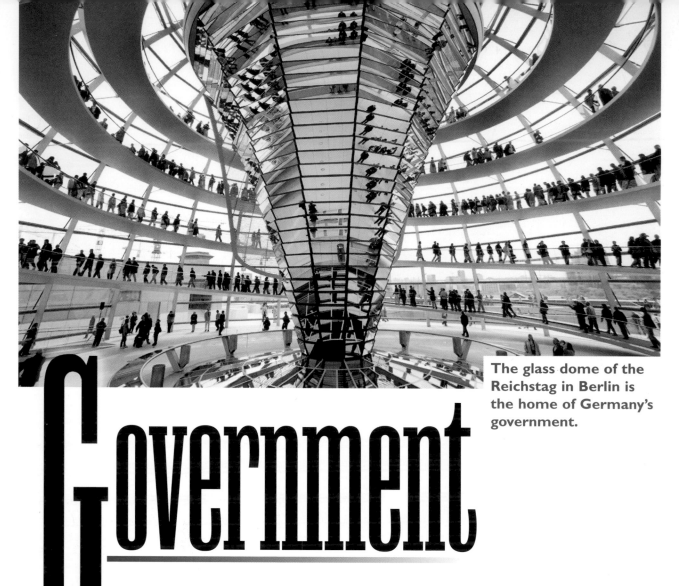

The glass dome of the Reichstag in Berlin is the home of Germany's government.

Government

Gerhard Schroeder

Germany's government is a **federal republic**. The current government has been in place only since 1990, when East and West Germany were **reunited**. In many ways, the German government is similar to the U.S. democracy. Gerhard Schroeder has served as Germany's **chancellor** since 1998. His duties are very much like those of a U.S. president. Elected leaders represent the citizens of Germany in two groups of lawmakers. These are known as the Federal Council and the Federal Assembly. They are like the U.S. Senate and House of Representatives.

People took pieces of the Berlin Wall as souvenirs when East and West Germany were reunited.

Construction of the Berlin Wall began in 1961.

History

Germany was divided into two sections after World War II ended in 1945. They sections were East Germany and West Germany.

West Germany adopted a democratic form of government. East Germany adopted **Communism**. It also developed ties with the **Soviet Union**.

East Germans felt that life was better in West Germany. Many of them began to move there. To stop them, the Communist government built a high wall through the city of Berlin. The Berlin Wall divided East and West Germany. They became one nation again in 1990.

Ludwig van Beethoven

Important People

Ludwig van Beethoven was born in Bonn in 1770. He is thought to be the greatest **composer** of **symphonies** who ever lived.

Caprice in February, a painting by Paul Klee

Clara Schumann is remembered as a brilliant concert pianist.

Germany has a rich musical history. Perhaps you know the names of these other greats from the world of classical music: Johann Sebastian Bach, Felix Mendelssohn, George Handel, Robert Schumann, Richard Wagner, Richard Strauss, and Johannes Brahms. All of them were German.

The artist Paul Klee spent the beginning and end of his life in Switzerland. He is especially remembered for the paintings he created during the years he lived in Germany. His works are an important part of the history of modern art.

Many Germans have jobs in manufacturing, such as this man. He is building a printing press.

Jobs

Many Germans have jobs manufacturing products, such as iron, steel, and chemicals, that are used in the country or are exported. People also work in banking and finance, insurance, and jobs related to tourism. They also own farms.

Hardworking people have helped to make Germany's economy one of the strongest in the world.

Keepsakes

How do you know if you have a real Steiff bear? It has a button sewn into one of its ears.

You can find special carved wooden clocks in the Black Forest region of southwestern Germany. More than 60 million clocks are made there each year. Many of them feature carvings of the cuckoo bird, which is why people often call them "cuckoo clocks."

Another great keepsake is the teddy bear. In 1904, Margarete Steiff and her company introduced the new toy at the World's Fair in St. Louis, Missouri. It became known as the teddy bear.

A craftsperson displays his beautifully carved clock.

Land · Fluss

(FLOOSS)
means river.

You can see many mountains, forests, and meadows in Germany. There are many rivers that flow through Germany, too.

Lake Gerold

Germany shares borders with nine other countries. Most of Germany's northern border is made up of its coastline along the North and Baltic Seas.

Then the land gently rises to form a region known as the Central Uplands. A beautiful mountain range known as the Alps forms Germany's southern border with the countries of France, Switzerland, and Austria.

Many rivers flow through Germany. They include the Elbe, the Rhine, the Main, and the Danube. The Danube is the second-longest river in Europe.

GERMANY

SWEDEN

DENMARK

Baltic Sea

North Sea

POLAND

Hamburg

Berlin ★

GERMANY

NETHERLANDS

Düsseldorf

BELGIUM

Rhine River

Frankfurt

CZECH
REPUBLIC

FRANCE

LUXEMBOURG

Map

Black
Forest

Danube River

Munich

Bavarian Alps

AUSTRIA

LIECHTENSTEIN

SWITZERLAND

MILES
0   150

KILOMETERS
0   150

ITALY

Nation

Fahne

(FAH-nuh)
means flag.

Three stripes of black, red, and gold make up the German flag. Just as Americans refer to their flag as the "red, white, and blue," the German flag is nicknamed the **schwarz, rot, gold** ("black, red, gold"). These three colors are the same as those on Germany's **coat of arms**. Each of the German states also has its own flag.

A traffic accident leaves motorists waiting on the Autobahn.

Only in Germany

The German **Autobahn** is the second-biggest roadway system in the world. The largest interstate highway system is in the United States.

Motorists on the Autobahn can change directions using the interchanges.

Construction of the Autobahn was begun under the direction of Adolf Hitler in 1933. Since that time, it has grown to include more than 6,500 miles (10, 450 km) of roadways. It connects all of Germany's major towns and cities.

A popular myth states that there is no speed limit on the Autobahn. This is not completely true. There are speed limit signs on many sections of the roadway. Still, drivers often travel the Autobahn at high speeds. Parts of the Autobahn extend into Austria and Switzerland, too. But those countries charge money, called tolls, for using the road.

A Bavarian farm family

People

This grandmother and her granddaughter live in northern Germany.

More than 82 million people live in Germany. It is the second-most populated country in Europe. Most German people live in cities. Workers from Turkey make up 2.5 percent of the population.

These houses are in Rothenburg, which is in southern Germany.

In southern Germany, some people live in older homes that look like pictures from a storybook. Many Germans own their own homes. Southern Germany has mountains that are good for skiing. The land is also very rich in natural resources, like coal and metals.

In northern Germany, many people live in cities. Some of them live in apartments. Northern Germany is good for fishing since it is near the coastline. Many companies ship goods from this part of Germany to other countries.

This young girl and boy are riding through the city.

Question

Is your dog German?

Many popular breeds of dogs come from Germany. There are schnauzers, dachshunds, doberman pinschers, German shepherds, and many others.

Giant schnauzers once herded cattle. Their smaller cousins, the miniature schnauzers, hunted rats. The earliest known picture of a schnauzer is in a five-hundred-year-old **tapestry**.

Dachshunds hunted badgers. Their long bodies are great for crawling into underground tunnels. Dogs such as Doberman pinschers, German shepherds, Weimaraners, German short-haired and wire-haired pointers herd animals, assist hunters, or guard homes and markets.

German wire-haired pointer

A painting of Martin Luther

Religion

The Cologne Cathedral is one of the world's most beautiful churches.

Around the year 1520, a German priest named Martin Luther began to complain to leaders of the Catholic Church. He did not think that rich people should be allowed to pay money to have their sins forgiven. He felt this meant that they did not truly feel sorry about their bad deeds. People who agreed with him started their own churches. These churches were called "Protestant" because they were formed as an act of protest. Today, there are more Protestants than Catholics living in Germany.

German students go to school for almost the whole year, even Saturdays!

School & Sports

German children begin school at about age six. They must remain in school until they are at least 15 years old. However, the school day ends in time for lunch, and students do homework in the afternoons. About one-fourth of Germany's students go to college.

Soccer is the team sport most often played in Germany, and there are many different professional and amateur teams. German athletes are also known for their skill in figure skating and skiing.

Germany competes in World Cup soccer.

Transportation

There are many kinds of transportation in Germany. Many
Germans own cars but there are other ways to get around, too.
How about the train or an airplane? Railway service is owned
and managed by the federal government. People can travel to
many German cities on trains. Lufthansa is the national airline.
Its airplanes fly to many countries.

Canals allow goods to be moved by barges and ships
between major waterways. The Kiel Canal connects the North
Sea with the Baltic Sea in the northern part of the country.

29

Unusual Places

Off the western coast of Denmark is a narrow strip of land called Sylt. No part of Germany is farther north than this. Its windy climate makes waves on the waters of the North Sea, so it is a popular spot with German surfers. It has health resorts that attract many famous people.

People have been coming to Sylt for centuries. There is a church there that is more than 900 years old! In the high **dunes** along the coast, you can visit a grave that is older than recorded history.

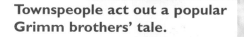
Townspeople act out a popular Grimm brothers' tale.

Visiting the Country

The Brothers Grimm

Don't forget to make stops along Fairy-Tale Road when you visit Germany. This 400-mile (640-km) trail connects the towns of Hanau and Bremen. Along the way, there are many things to see that are associated with Jakob and Wilhelm Grimm. The Brothers Grimm are the authors of popular stories like *Snow White*, *Sleeping Beauty*, and *The Pied Piper of Hamelin*. At the Brothers Grimm Museum in Kassel, you can see original editions of their most popular fairy tales.

31

Members of a Hitler Youth group during one of their regular marches.

Window to the Past

Adolf Hitler became Germany's leader during the 1930s. His actions brought about World War II and caused the deaths of millions of people.

Adolf Hitler is shown in the background of this poster for Hitler Youth.

Hitler wanted everyone in Germany to believe in the same things. He formed an organization called Hitler Youth. Its members were boys between the ages of 13 and 17. For girls, he formed the League of German Maidens. Marching and other physical fitness activities forced young people to work together and to think in the same ways. They were encouraged to spy on their neighbors and families.

Lowenberg Castle was built to look much older than it really is.

Frankenstein Castle is near Darmstadt.

X-tra Special Things

Among the most spectacular sights in Germany are the country's many castles. Some of them were built centuries ago to protect kings from their enemies.

The Great Hall in Neuschwanstein Castle

Thousands of tourists visit Neuschwanstein Castle each year.

Linderhof Castle was also built by Ludwig II.

However, Germany's most amazing castles were never used for defense and are not very old. They were built by Ludwig II, who became king of Bavaria in 1864. Ludwig II had a wonderful imagination. One of the castles he had built is Neuschwanstein Castle, which sits high on the top of a mountain. It was the model for Sleeping Beauty's castle at Disneyland.

Witch costumes are popular during Fasching.

Dinkelsbuhl pageant participants

Berlin's Santa Parade

Yearly Festivals

Munich is famous for the harvest celebration known as *Oktoberfest*. It is the world's largest festival. More than seven million people attend.

Beer arrives for Oktoberfest on decorated, horse-drawn wagons.

Fasching is the German version of Carnival or Mardi Gras. It lasts for several days during the winter. People have fun dressing in costumes and dancing in the streets before the quiet **Lenten** season begins.

May Day is a holiday that celebrates the coming of spring. In Germany, it is also a day that honors workers, much like Labor Day does in the United States and Canada.

A beautiful pageant at the annual Dinkelsbuhl Children's Festival tells the story of how children brought an end to a battle long ago.

Maypoles are part of the May Day celebration.

These cones are filled with school supplies, candy and other gifts!

Zuckertuete

Zuckertuete is a word that means "sugar bag." Schultueten is another name for a zuckertuete. It is a very special gift that German children receive on the first day of school. Large, cone-shaped bags are filled with candy, school supplies, and other gifts. A zuckertuete may be as large as 3 feet (1 m) in length. Parents give them to their children to remind them that education is important.

■ German and English Words

Autobahn A connected series of highways in Germany

chamois A type of antelope found in the mountainous regions of Europe

chancellor (CHAN-suh-lur) The leader of the German government

coat of arms A symbol that represents a group of people, usually appearing on a banner

Communism (KOM-yuh-niz-uhm) A type of government that attempts to make all citizens equal, but often causes them to live under harsh rules and conditions

composer (kuhm-POZ-uhr) A person that writes music

dirndl A traditional dress worn by women and girls

dunes Hills of sand usually found near the shores of an ocean or a large lake

European Union A group of countries, including Germany, with shared national goals

Fasching A German festival that happens before the start of Lent

federal republic A type of government that is made up of states or districts within a larger national government

herd (HURD) A large group of animals

lederhosen Short leather pants with suspenders worn by men and boys

Lenten A period of about eight weeks during which Christians prepare for Easter

Middle Ages A period of history from about A.D. 400 to 1400

Oktoberfest A harvest festival held in late September, known especially for beer-drinking

porcelain Delicate, white ceramic dishes, plates, or decorative items

reunited When two things that have been separated are put back together

schwarz, rot, gold German words for *black, red, and gold*; a term for the German flag

schultueten Another name for a *zuckertuete*

Soviet Union A Communist country that existed from 1917 to 1991 and included Russia and fourteen other nations, which are now independent

symphony (SIM-fuh-nee) A long musical composition written for an orchestra to perform

tapestry A picture that is made by weaving or sewing different colors of thread together to form a design

tusks (TUHSKS) Teeth that grow from the corners of the mouths of elephants, wild boars, and other animals

zuckertuete A cone-shaped container that holds candy and school supplies

■ Let's Explore More

Cooking the German Way by Helga Parnell, Lerner Publications, 2003

Germany by Susan Heinrichs Gray, Children's Press, 2003

Look What Came from Germany by Kevin A. Davis, Franklin Watts, 2000

Websites

http://www.germany-info.org
Click on the "Germany for Kids" link to be connected to a young person's guide to the country.

http://library.thinkquest.org/26576
This site offers additional recipes for German foods, a complete list of German holidays and festivals, recordings of music by German composers, and more.

Index

Italic page numbers indicate illustrations.

Meet the Author

JEFF REYNOLDS was raised on a farm in Illinois. He has lived in Minneapolis-St. Paul, New York City, and Connecticut, and now lives and works in Washington, D.C. He received a B.A. from Western Illinois University and an M.A. in Theater History and Criticism from Brooklyn College. At various times he has been a farmer, milk man, school custodian, housepainter, hotel bellman, stamp dealer, teacher, librarian, actor, journalist, and editor. He is also the author of A to Z books about Germany, Japan, Puerto Rico, and the United States.